Christina Aguilera

Biography

From Mickey Mouse to Pop Legend

Shawn V. Orr

Table of content

Introduction

Few could have predicted Christina Aguilera's influence on mainstream music and society when she first appeared on television in the late 1990s. Aguilera reinvented what it meant to be a pop star by breaking boundaries with her powerful voice, unwavering resolve, and desire for self-expression. Her career has impacted millions of people, solidifying her position as a generational voice via her unadulterated skill, constant reinvention, and unrelenting commitment to her craft.

Christina's career was full of challenges, unexpected turns, and unquestionable victories, starting with her early days on *The Mickey Mouse Club* with other future superstars. In a music industry dominated by boy bands and pop princesses, her first song, "Genie in a Bottle," swiftly became a worldwide hit and established her as a strong new voice. However, Christina defied convention and pushed the bounds of creativity instead of taking the conventional route. In addition to her skill as a vocalist, she gained notoriety for her dedication to honesty, her fearless approach to self-empowerment concerns, and her readiness to be vulnerable with her audience. Aguilera has continuously opted to change rather than fit in throughout her career. She gained creative autonomy and was able to express very intimate feelings via her music with her landmark album *Stripped*. Songs like "Beautiful" struck a chord with listeners of all ages, becoming hymns to fortitude and self-acceptance. She experimented with many genres, refined her persona, and confronted criticism head-on, coming out stronger every time. Aguilera is now a symbol of empowerment in addition to her musical accomplishments. Her story illustrates the difficulties of celebrity, the struggles of self-discovery, and the victory of being loyal to one's voice in the face of an industry that is always evolving. Younger artists are also influenced by her, since they see her as a pioneer in the fields of creative independence and self-determination.

Christina Aguilera: From Mickey Mouse to Pop Legend is a biography that explores the life and career of a lady who defied categorisation, tracing her journey from a child star to a pop icon who still inspires people today. Here, we honor Christina Aguilera's voice, talent, and tenacity, which have contributed to her status as an icon for more than 20 years.

Chapter 1: Early Beginnings

Born on Staten Island, New York, on December 18, 1980, Christina María Aguilera grew up in a household where music was more than simply a hobby, it was a way of life. Christina was enthralled with the prospect of performing from an early age. Christina's early admiration for strong singers like Etta James and Billie Holiday was shaped by her mother, a musician herself, who exposed her to vintage soul and jazz recordings. Christina started to dream of a career in music as she listened to their heartfelt voices, seeing herself as a vocalist who could touch people's emotions. Singing provided Aguilera with an escape from the turbulent home she grew up in. Her upbringing was made more unstable by the repeated moves she experienced as a result of her father's military profession. Singing became a lifeline throughout these formative years. Christina's family and anybody who heard her sing saw that she had a vocal ability that was much above her years as she found her voice. She stood out from her friends because of her early capacity to express unfiltered emotion.

Aguilera started doing local talent contests when she was eight years old, quickly becoming known as "the little girl with the big voice." She pursued further possibilities as a result of her exceptional performances, and in 1993, at the age of twelve, she became a member of *The All New Mickey Mouse Club*. Christina performed on stage with Britney Spears, Ryan Gosling, and Justin Timberlake, making this Disney program a breeding ground for future pop stars. Christina's brilliance was evident among her co-stars despite her youth. She impressed both the audience and her co-stars with her vocal strength and composure, even delivering Aretha Franklin's "Respect" in one performance. In addition to giving her a taste of professional show business, *The Mickey Mouse Club* was a pivotal moment in her life because it helped her comprehend the expectations of celebrity.

But there were pressures associated with the event. Christina sometimes felt out of place since her large voice was not always seen as appropriate for the format of the program. She knew even as a preteen that her demeanour and voice were unique, a quality that would later become both a strength and a challenge. Christina was left with bigger goals and a sense of being on the brink of something great when *The Mickey Mouse Club* was canceled in 1994, but she had no idea how to get there.

It's seldom easy to go from kid star to pop musician, and Christina's experience was no exception. She returned to a more subdued existence after *The Mickey Mouse Club*, but she was not happy to remain out of the limelight. She started practicing, creating demo tapes, and auditioning because she was determined to get into the music business. Frequently informed she was too young or didn't match the late 1990s pop scene's mold, which was quickly being overtaken by more polished, meticulously marketed acts she endured many rejections. In 1998, she recorded "Reflection" for Disney's animated film *Mulan*, which marked a turning point in her career. The song restored her reputation with music professionals and demonstrated her singing prowess. She demonstrated that she possessed the emotional depth and vocal strength to enthral an audience with her first significant release. Because "Reflection" was so successful, Christina was able to get a recording deal with RCA Records, which paved the way for her first album. The song was more than simply a success; it was a statement of the kind of artist she wanted to be: powerful, passionate, and not afraid to be different. Christina had evolved from a child star to a young lady prepared to take on the music business and, as she would soon demonstrate, upend it from the ground up.

Early in life, Christina Aguilera shown a combination of skill, drive, and fortitude. She was prepared for her future profession by these early experiences on *The Mickey Mouse Club*, at her childhood home, and at local talent shows. She had known the pleasures of performing as well as the difficulties of being unique in a field that often encourages uniformity. Christina was prepared to enter the music business on her own terms thanks to her unique voice and her developing self-awareness. The world had no idea that this bashful girl with a loud voice would soon rise to prominence as one of pop music's most vibrant and significant performers. At this early point in her career, Christina Aguilera was about to go on a journey that would change the face of contemporary

music forever, turning her from a young dreamer to a
pop icon.

Chapter 2: Breaking into the Music Scene

After signing a recording deal with RCA Records, Christina Aguilera had the difficult challenge of putting together a first album that would showcase her distinct voice to the world. Aguilera was motivated to leave her mark despite her youth and relative unknown status in the music world. Her innate ability to sing let her stand out right away, unlike many other performers, but she was also breaking into a field that required not only skill but also a well-cultivated persona. Christina soon discovered, however, that success would not be simple. Although they saw her talent, record executives had a certain idea of her that reflected the bubblegum music that was becoming popular thanks to artists like Britney Spears and the Backstreet Boys. Christina was appreciative of the chance, but she had to balance the industry's expectations of her with her creative integrity. To make her self-titled first album, she worked with producers and composers for hours in the recording studio. She was young, ready to show herself, and prepared to put in a lot of effort to live up to the high standards set for her. However, despite her commitment, there were some frustrating aspects of the procedure. Although she was often counselled to adopt a lighter, more commercial style, she wanted her record to highlight her vocal range and emotional depth. Self-expression and the needs of the industry have to be balanced.

Aguilera's first single, "Genie in a Bottle," was released in August 1999 and quickly gained popularity. Her status as a new pop sensation was cemented when the song swiftly rose to the top of the Billboard Hot 100 rankings. Aguilera's seductive voice and the song's infectious, light-hearted rhythm made it popular with listeners around. The popular song "Genie in a Bottle" established her as a pop star while also teasing the breadth of her vocal prowess. Soon after, she released her first album, *Christina Aguilera*, which became an immediate hit. The album showcased her vocal power and variety by combining heartfelt ballads with appealing pop tunes. Songs like "Come On Over Baby (All I Want Is You)" and "What a Girl Wants" were immediate successes, catapulting her to the top of the charts and gaining her global fame. Her status as one of the most promising new talents of her time was cemented in 2000 when the album sold millions of copies worldwide and won her the Grammy Award for Best New Artist.

Despite Christina Aguilera's financial success, her status as a pop princess dominated the public's opinion of her. She seemed to many to be simply another pop star in a sea of youthful, blond, and vivacious female vocalists. Christina, however, was resolved to dispel this myth and present her own artistic voice and individuality. She had an increasing desire to show a more genuine and intimate side of herself since she understood she had more to give than the superficial picture her first album had produced. Christina Aguilera was thrown into the limelight like never before as a result of her sudden stardom. She was no longer the little girl who sang on *The Mickey Mouse Club* or in talent events. She was now well-known and often the subject of media attention. Her whole life was on exhibit, including her personal relationships and fashion choices.

Christina battled the constraints of her public image. She was thankful for her success, but she struggled to balance the pop star persona that had been created for her with who she really was. As a counterbalance to the more controversial Britney Spears, she was dubbed the "good girl" of pop and was urged to keep up this polished, innocent appearance. Aguilera, however, secretly yearned for artistic independence and the opportunity to express herself more truthfully. She started to feel a lot of pressure to fit in, and she knew that if she wanted to have a successful career on her terms, something had to change. She felt a strong need to be authentic since her encounters with fans served as another reminder of the influence her music has. Christina quickly became well-known, and her performances were packed with admirers who were moved by her voice and song. However, this public admiration also came with pressure to meet the standards set by the business, her company, and her fans. Christina started to feel that her polished persona didn't really represent who she was when she went on tour and marketed her record. She wanted to explore her music more deeply and provide a genuine representation of her personal hardships and experiences.

Aguilera was irritated with the restrictions imposed on her as the tornado of celebrity persisted. Beyond the whimsical themes of adolescent love and innocence, she wanted to sing about subjects that spoke to her. Christina was a lady with sentiments to share, tales to tell, and a desire to utilise music to reach a wider audience. Even though her early success was satisfying, she wished she had more creative control over her profession. Christina started to separate herself from the persona that had been created for her at this point. She began experimenting with other genres and finding inspiration in performers she liked, like Janis Joplin, Nina Simone and Etta James, singers who were not only fearless in their use of emotion and vocal prowess, but also unafraid to push boundaries. Aguilera aimed to produce meaningful music that represented her own experience and the difficulties she had encountered. It wasn't an easy road to creative independence. Christina's record company opposed her because they were concerned that a significant shift in her persona would turn off her fans. They saw her as a mainstream pop sensation, therefore they were hesitant to take her into more complex and contentious areas. Aguilera, however, was adamant. She was aware that she would become less of herself if she kept fitting in. This insight signaled a sea change in her career and prepared the way for *Stripped*, her subsequent album that would reshape her sound, image, and legacy.

Christina Aguilera's first album's success catapulted her to global fame, but it also left her craving more freedom, more honesty, and more chances to express herself freely. Millions of people had taken notice of her singing abilities, but she had not yet disclosed who she really was as an artist. Christina was aware that her career in music was only getting started as she was ready to move on from the success of her debut. She was prepared to take big chances, to defy herself and the expectations of the business, and to establish herself as an artist who would be recognised for her bravery and genuineness in addition to her voice. She had no idea that her next record would break boundaries, alter preconceptions, and make her a well-known voice in the music industry for resilience, independence, and empowerment. This turning point in her career served as a reminder that her narrative and voice were destined for something more than pop success. Christina Aguilera was prepared to change, to stop being a "pop princess," and to become a performer whose message would be remembered for years to come.

Chapter 3: Reinvention with "Stripped"

Christina Aguilera had experienced the euphoria of success and celebrity with her first album by 2002, but she believed that the "pop princess" stereotype had hindered her creativity. Aguilera started a daring reinvention quest because she was determined to overcome the constraints of the business. She set out to investigate themes of perseverance, self-expression, vulnerability, and strength with her second album, *Stripped*. She would take complete creative charge this time, making sure that her voice was recognised.

Christina has never done *Stripped* like this before. She composed songs that were honest, unvarnished, and very personal while collaborating closely with producers like Alicia Keys, Linda Perry, and Scott Storch. She put her own experiences into the lyrics, tackling subjects that were seldom discussed in mainstream music at the time, embracing self-worth, and facing anxieties. Anthems such as "Fighter," "Beautiful," and "Can't Hold Us Down" each conveyed a distinct message of strength and perseverance. It was difficult to take these imaginative chances. Aguilera encountered opposition from her label, who feared that fans would become disenchanted with her departure from her polished persona. Christina, however, was determined to have her music represent who she really was, even if it meant taking chances. For her, the procedure was life-changing, a watershed in both her work and identity as an artist.

With the publication of *Stripped*, Aguilera became a more confident and self-assured person. She adopted a raw and unabashed style, rejecting the norms of a well manicured image. The alter identity "Xtina" enabled Christina to explore her darker, uncensored side, and she donned edgy clothes and dyed her hair black. Many of her followers were taken aback by this shift in her appearance and demeanour, and others criticised her for allegedly straying from her "good girl" persona. However, this was the first time that Aguilera was free from the limitations of the business to be who she really was. Pop, R&B, rock, and soul were among the many musical genres represented on *Stripped*. By embracing her sexuality and defying social expectations with songs like "Dirrty," Aguilera broke free from the constrictive stereotype of female pop artists. The contentious music video for the song, which included gritty, provocative images, caused a media frenzy. Aguilera defended her artistic decisions, seeing them as a celebration of her autonomy and control over her own body, despite criticism that she was attempting to be controversial for attention. The record, however, covered her experiences with suffering, self-acceptance, and inner power in addition to violating sexual limits. In Linda Perry's song "Beautiful," Christina gave one of her most emotional performances. The song's message of inner beauty and self-worth struck a deep chord with listeners everywhere, especially those who were having a hard time accepting and believing in themselves. Reaching listeners of all ages and ethnicities, "Beautiful" evolved become an anthem for inclusiveness and self-love. Its popularity not only made *Stripped* a seminal record, but it also made Aguilera a voice for many who felt excluded or misunderstood.

Aguilera's daring new identity and *Stripped's* thought-provoking themes were not overlooked. The media, journalists, and even some fans scrutinized her closely because they didn't like her transition from an innocent pop star to an opinionated performer. By juxtaposing her edgy appearance with the more refined and clean personalities of her colleagues, the media often portrayed her as the "bad girl" of pop and contrasted her to other female singers, such as Britney Spears. Discussions about women's empowerment and freedom of speech were triggered by Aguilera's decision to publicly embrace her sexuality. Christina was troubled by the criticism, but it strengthened her determination. She was aware that taking chances might result in criticism, yet she persisted in her conviction that she had to be herself. Songs like "Can't Hold Us Down," in particular, were her way of responding to her detractors. The double standards that women encounter in the music business, particularly with regard to sexuality and self-expression, were clearly addressed in the song. Aguilera made a strong statement about her freedom to define herself according to her own standards with songs that questioned society's critical gaze. Millions of listeners connected with *Stripped* despite the uproar, finding strength in her songs and identifying with her problems. The record became multi-platinum globally after receiving both critical and financial acclaim. Its influence extended beyond music, as it sparked pop culture conversations about gender, appearance, and self-expression. By effectively redefining herself, Aguilera demonstrated that she was an artist with a voice that mattered and that she was more than simply a pop star.

For Aguilera, making *Stripped* was a profoundly emotional voyage of self-discovery in addition to a career breakthrough. She was able to face her history, recover from traumatic events, and regain her identity as a result of the process. She had been under pressure for years to be "perfect," to fit into a mould, but with *Stripped*, she gave herself permission to explore her inner power, her imperfections, and her fears. Her battles with self-image, her experiences with trauma, and her quest for personal development were among the subjects she was able to address via the album. In songs like "Walk Away" and "I'm OK," she spoke candidly about the difficulties she had encountered, especially her tense relationship with her father. *Stripped* served as a therapeutic outlet for Christina, allowing her to face her suffering and turn it into art that could motivate others. Christina would continue on this path of self-discovery for the duration of her professional life. Her conviction that being genuine was worth the risk was confirmed by *Stripped's* popularity, and it served as a compass for her subsequent work. She no longer felt compelled to live up to the expectations of others. Knowing that her followers appreciated her openness and sensitivity just as much as her voice, she instead welcomed the opportunity to change.

Stripped had a long-lasting effect on the music business and was a turning point in Christina Aguilera's career. Because of the album's popularity and Aguilera's unreserved attitude to self-expression, subsequent musicians, particularly women were encouraged to embrace their uniqueness and talk candidly about their personal hardships. *Stripped* defied pop music conventions, demonstrating that popular music may be both financially successful and creatively bold. The work of several artists who came after Aguilera, such as Lady Gaga and Demi Lovato, demonstrates the impact of

Stripped. They point to her courage in expressing herself and her willingness to take on challenging subjects as sources of inspiration. For both her admirers and her colleagues, Aguilera's ability to remain true to herself in the face of heavy criticism served as a potent example of perseverance. With *Stripped,* Christina transformed herself from a pop artist to a cultural icon, a voice for empowerment, and a supporter of individual expression. This period of her life cemented her legacy by demonstrating to the world that she was a formidable presence, not just because of her vocal ability but also because of her bravery in being herself. Aguilera had been able to shed the label of "pop princess" and come out as a performer who would keep changing and speaking her mind.

Christina realised that this was just the start of a lifetime of development, discovery, and reinvention as she looked to the future. *Stripped* had freed her, and she would keep reinventing herself with every step, remaining loyal to the voice that had motivated millions worldwide.

Chapter 4: The Rise of a True Icon

Christina Aguilera was thrust into a whole new sphere of fame with the success of *Stripped*. She had established herself as a worldwide sensation and received critical praise, solidifying her legacy in pop culture. *Stripped* changed the game by allowing her to deviate from the conventional pop world's expectations. She was now seen as an artist with a distinct voice who was not afraid to express her mind, rather than merely a pop singer. But this kind of celebrity also came with more scrutiny. The media followed Aguilera everywhere, with tabloids often covering her personal life and fashion choices. Aguilera maintained her concentration on her craft and her ambition to continue developing despite the demands of notoriety. She was aware that in order to be relevant in a field that was changing all the time, she would need to keep changing. In the near future, she would experiment with other genres, taking chances that would keep her in the public eye, but always on her terms.

Aguilera took a risk in 2006 when she released *Back to Basics*, her third album, which once again revolutionized her sound and image. Drawing inspiration from jazz, blues, and soul music from the 1920s to the 1950s, she incorporated a vintage style into her sound and imagery. The CD paid homage to the timeless musicians like Etta James, Billie Holiday, and Nina Simone who had influenced her as a young child. Working with producers like Mark Ronson, DJ Premier, and Linda Perry, Aguilera created an album that was both nostalgic and new by fusing modern sounds with old influences. *Back to Basics* further showcased Aguilera's flexibility while departing from the harsh, urban vibe of *Stripped*. "Ain't No Other Man" and "Candyman" were two lead songs that demonstrated her remarkable vocal range and ability to capture a bygone atmosphere while still producing successes that reached the top of the charts. In addition to winning her another Grammy, "Ain't No Other Man" became an immediate classic, proving that Aguilera was not just a formidable voice but also a smart performer who wasn't hesitant to try new things. Her appearance changed once more. In homage to legendary actresses of the past, she embraced platinum locks, scarlet lipstick, and pin-up attire, adopting a beautiful, vintage

Hollywood look. Aguilera was able to explore a different facet of her artistic abilities via this reinvention, honouring the ladies who had before her and securing her own position in the tradition of powerful female artists. This new look was welcomed by her fans, and *Back to Basics* was a critical and financial triumph, demonstrating that one of Aguilera's best qualities was her courage to take chances.

Aguilera's personal life underwent substantial adjustments at this time. She wed Jordan Bratman, a music marketing professional, in 2005, and the two of them had their first child, a boy called Max, in 2008. Aguilera's life and outlook took on new depth after becoming a mother, which affected her priorities and songs. She often spoke about the happiness of motherhood and how it altered her perspective, which further inspired her to serve as a powerful role model for her followers. However, Aguilera's personal experiences weren't without difficulties, just like any life in the spotlight. Her marriage suffered as a result of the demands of her job, family life, and celebrity, and she and Bratman finally got divorced in 2010. Aguilera found this time challenging as she dealt with the heartache of a public separation and tried to juggle her job and motherhood. Despite these personal struggles, Aguilera found strength in music and performance and used them to express her feelings in her art. She started tackling themes of resiliency and self-worth with even more conviction when her experiences with love, pregnancy, and grief gave her songs even more depth. As she developed more as an artist and a person, these ideas would play a major role in her subsequent endeavours.

Acting presented Aguilera with a new challenge in 2010. She played a teenage singer from a rural village who relocates to Los Angeles to follow her aspirations in the musical film *Burlesque*, co-starring with Cher. With songs that blended jazz, pop, and cabaret elements, the role gave Aguilera a new platform to display her vocal prowess. Aguilera's performance and the music were acclaimed despite the film's mixed reviews; songs like "Show Me How You Burlesque" and "Express" became favourites among fans. Aguilera was able to expand her creative talents and develop a fresh respect for on-screen performance thanks to the experience, which offered her a taste of acting. At around the same time, Aguilera started a new endeavor in 2011 when she became a coach on *The Voice*. The show was a huge success, and Aguilera was able to reach a new generation of budding musicians via her work as a coach. She was able to connect with fans more personally because to her involvement on *The Voice*, which demonstrated her skill and dedication to developing talent. She was often commended for her abilities to coach competitors, offering insightful counsel drawn on her own experiences in the field. Outside of her music, *The Voice* became one of her most enduring and well-known endeavors, reintroducing her to the public in a new, empowered capacity. In addition to being a teaching experience, her appearance on *The Voice* highlighted her status as an icon who has opened doors for up-and-coming musicians. Christina's career longevity and the respect she had in the business were shown by her transformation from child star to mentor for up-and-coming talent. Her love of music and her desire to help others find their path, as she had, were mirrored in her enthusiasm for mentoring up-and-coming vocalists.

Lotus, Aguilera's seventh studio album, was released in 2012. The record symbolized her strength and tenacity, a "rebirth" after all of the ups and downs she had gone through. *Lotus* had strong, uplifting songs like "Army of Me" and "Let There Be Love," which expressed her inner strength and optimism, despite not being as economically successful as her earlier albums. She termed the CD a celebration of her journey, reflecting her perseverance and capacity to rise above adversities. Aguilera took a break from music after *Lotus* to concentrate on her family and personal life, but she continued to be involved in the business via *The Voice* and other partnerships. She kept experimenting with her sound and style, and in 2018 she made a comeback with the album *Liberation*, which represented yet another reinvention. Aguilera was able to rediscover her passion for soulful, experimental music with the daring, contemplative album *Liberation*. Singles like "Fall in Line" starring Demi Lovato, which emphasized the value of female strength and perseverance, helped it get praise from critics. *Liberation* served as a reminder of Aguilera's development as an artist and her dedication to making music that was both powerful and intimate.

Christina Aguilera's impact on the music business changed along with her career. Her transformation from pop princess to strong, versatile performer has served as an inspiration to other artists who admire her bravery, sincerity, and vocal prowess. Other artists, especially women, who struggle to strike a balance between their own identities and professional standards, have benefited from her courage to speak her truth, push boundaries, and take chances. Christina's influence extends beyond her songs. She is now a representation of the qualities she has always espoused: self-expression, independence, and tenacity. She dispelled myths, confronted detractors, and repeatedly reinvented herself, demonstrating to the world that genuine artwork is about development, genuineness, and being loyal to oneself. Aguilera's legacy is safe as she travels farther. She continues to be a cherished symbol, an advocate for self-determination, and an encouragement to others who dare to be unique. Christina Aguilera's tale is not just one of achievement;

it also serves as a tribute to the value of following one's heart, no matter where it takes one, and the strength of self-discovery.

Chapter 5: The Evolution of an Icon

Following a short break and the release of *Lotus*, Christina Aguilera's 2018 comeback to music with *Liberation* marked a turning point in her career. *Liberation* was a project of self-discovery and empowerment after years of experimenting with many facets of her personality and creative spectrum. This album, in contrast to her previous work, combined deep ballads, hip-hop, and R&B with reflective lyrics that let Aguilera show her true self. The album, which provided a sensitive glimpse into her life and challenges as well as her victories and changes, was her most intimate effort to date. Working with a variety of musicians, such as Anderson Paak and Kanye West, Aguilera produced an album that stretched boundaries and praised her creative independence. Songs like her duet with Demi Lovato, "Fall in Line," which addressed themes of gender inequity and social pressures on young women, became anthems for women standing up for their value. While songs like "Like I Do" embraced contemporary production without sacrificing her vocal creativity,

"Twice" and "Maria" demonstrated her vocal depth and emotional complexity.

Liberation demonstrated Aguilera's development and maturity in addition to being a musical return. By striking a balance between the ferocity of *Stripped* and the sophisticated craftsmanship of *Back to Basics*, it demonstrated to her admirers that she had fully returned. *Liberation* served as a reminder to Christina that she still had the ability to control her story and that her voice could captivate audiences, motivating a new generation of listeners.

Aguilera has advocated for women's rights, LGBTQ+ rights, and humanitarian causes throughout her career, speaking out on topics that are important to her. As her platform expanded, she spoke out on social and political concerns and partnered her company with other causes, using her power to change the world. Her advocacy work became an integral part of who she was, supporting her message of resilience and self-determination. Aguilera has shown her dedication to utilising her position for good via her involvement with the United Nations World Food Programme and her support of several organisations. She has publicly supported equal rights and often dedicates her shows to her LGBTQ+ fans, demonstrating her support for the LGBTQ+ community. Her steadfast support of LGBTQ+ issues earned her the Human Rights Campaign's 2019 "Ally for Equality" award, demonstrating her dedication to acceptance and inclusiveness. Her generosity reflects her own ideals and her desire to give back, and it goes beyond her public character. She has a unique perspective on the value of compassion, perseverance, and self-worth because of her past, which started with difficulties and hardship. Beyond only her music, Aguilera is a force for social change and empowerment, demonstrating to her followers that compassion and strength can coexist.

Aguilera started her Las Vegas residency at the Zappos Theatre in 2019 with a concert called *The Xperience*, in which she celebrated her career, artistic development, and growth. *The Xperience* was more than just a performance for Aguilera; it was an opportunity to reunite with her fans, revisit her greatest successes, and highlight her artistic development. The presentation showcased her evolution over the years and included aspects from her whole career, from *Genie in a Bottle* to *Liberation*. Aguilera was able to combine her passion for theater, costumes and narrative into the lavish, eye-catching residency. Every performance was designed to honour her favourite songs and creative periods while guiding fans through her career and development. Aguilera showed throughout the residency that she was still a formidable performer who could enthrall crowds with her passion, charm, and unrivaled vocals. *The Xperience* served as a reminder of Aguilera's lasting influence as well as a celebration of her accomplishments. It gave her the chance to think back on her journey with her fans and showed that she could adjust and flourish in the ever-evolving music industry. The residency was well received by critics, highlighting her reputation as one of pop's most recognisable and adaptable performers.

Christina Aguilera's ability to reinvent herself while adhering to her creative vision has been a defining characteristic of her career. Aguilera has shown that her development is both personal and professional, going from the youthful pop sensation of *Genie in a Bottle* to the courageous and daring artist of *Stripped*, the glitzy diva of *Back to Basics*, and the strong woman of *Liberation*. The many phases of her life are reflected in her music, with each album representing a new phase in her tale of resiliency and development. Aguilera has had a significant impact on the music business. By shattering preconceptions, she opened the door for other artists to embrace their uniqueness, voice their opinions on social concerns, and take charge of their own creative process. Generations of artists have been encouraged to be unabashedly themselves by her daring approach to self-expression. She is still well-respected in the field today, not just for her ability to speak, but also for having the guts to stand up for what she believes in. Her influence extends beyond her songs. Aguilera has become as a cultural icon, representing honesty and self-determination. While remaining loyal to her artistic vision, she has persevered despite criticism, personal struggles, and industry barriers. Aguilera's path is proof of the strength of perseverance, self-belief, and the readiness to change.

Aguilera's enthusiasm for music and creativity hasn't waned as she looks to the future. She keeps making references to next endeavours, teamwork, and even a possible comeback to acting. Her admirers are anticipating her next chapter with great anticipation since they are excited about what is ahead. Aguilera is far from finished with her path, she keeps pushing the envelope and redefining what it means to be an artist in the modern world. She has had a remarkable transformation from a teenage pop singer to a music legend, and her strength and resilience are shown by her capacity to evolve, adapt, and connect with her fans. Aguilera continues to be an influential figure in the field as she goes ahead, serving as a constant reminder that genuine creativity involves accepting change and being loyal to oneself.

Christina Aguilera is now a multifaceted artist and an empowerment icon, surpassing her original reputation as a pop singer. She has established herself as one of the most significant voices of her age by her unwavering devotion to social causes, her passion for music, and her never-ending desire to improve herself. Her tale of tenacity, ingenuity, and self-discovery encourages millions of others to be authentically themselves. Christina Aguilera is a living example of the power of reinvention as she sets off on the next phase of her journey. She demonstrates that anybody can succeed and leave a lasting legacy if they possess bravery, honesty, and a ferocious resolve.

Chapter 6: Redefining Pop Stardom in the Digital Era

Christina Aguilera was once again forced to adjust to a quickly changing music business as it entered the era of streaming, social media, and direct fan interactions. The new period was characterised by fast access to music, streaming platforms, and a continual digital presence, while the early days of her career were dominated by CD sales, MTV music videos, and conventional radio play. Given her existing fan base and reputation, Aguilera had to adjust to these changes by figuring out how to engage with both her devoted following and a new generation that was used to YouTube, Instagram, and TikTok. Aguilera's readiness to adopt new trends and technology while being loyal to her heritage was one of her strong points. Aguilera made her whole discography accessible on all of the main streaming services when streaming started to take over, guaranteeing that her music was heard by people all over the world. She started to use social media more often, posting updates about her life, interacting with admirers, and promoting her art on sites like Instagram and Twitter. Aguilera was able to cross the generational divide by addressing younger listeners who had grown up in a very different environment from the one in which her career started because of her openness and readiness to speak with her audience directly.

An era of more cross-genre artist collaborations was also brought about by the digital age. This setting was ideal for Christina Aguilera, who is renowned for her ability to combine genres and sing well. She started working with a range of musicians, broadening her musical horizons and discovering new sounds. She demonstrated her flexibility by working with Pitbull, Maroon 5, A Great Big World, and Demi Lovato, reaching audiences in pop, EDM, soul, and even independent music. The Latin music scene was one of her most well-known recent partnerships. Aguilera has always been a multilingual singer who has embraced her Latin ancestry; in 2022, she released an album in Spanish called *La Fuerza*. Through this endeavour, Aguilera explored ranchera, bachata, and reggaeton rhythms while re-establishing a connection with her Latin fanbase. She was able to develop her artistic abilities while respecting her heritage thanks to *La Fuerza*, which also brought her in front of a new audience who found great resonance in the genuineness of her cultural expression. Aguilera proved via collaborations and genre-bending that she was not just a historical figure but also a contemporary musician who could thrive in the present musical environment. She was able to keep up her reputation as a vibrant force in the business by being receptive to new sounds and genres.

Fans had never-before-seen access to their favourite artists thanks to social media, and Aguilera's legacy expanded as her influence reached a new generation of musicians. As newer celebrities like Demi Lovato, Ariana Grande, and Miley Cyrus identified her as an inspiration, her effect on pop music, fashion, and self-expression became more apparent. For musicians navigating the challenges of popularity in the internet age, Aguilera's pioneering attitude served as a model, particularly in encouraging female artists to embrace their voices and authenticity. Beyond only music, Aguilera had an effect on social and cultural discussions about gender, empowerment, and self-expression. Her appearance and songs sparked conversations about perseverance, body positivity, and mental health, subjects that her fans and the larger online community often emphasized on social media. Through her career, Aguilera demonstrated how a pop singer can transform from a teenage hero to a revered figure who has a significant influence on social problems and society.

As evidence of her ongoing appeal and the devotion of her global fan base, Aguilera went on *The X Tour* in 2019, her first European tour in more than 13 years. The tour gave her the opportunity to play in front of crowds that had grown up with her music and celebrated her whole career, from her early songs to her more current work. Many fans found the tour to be nostalgic, but it was also an opportunity to see Aguilera at her best, giving strong performances that highlighted her showmanship and vocal skills. Aguilera's relationship with her fans, many of whom had followed her since her debut, was emphasized by *The X Tour*. As she recognised the path she had traveled and the individuals who had helped her along the way, the trip also included times for introspection and appreciation. It served as a reminder of Aguilera's importance in the mainstream music industry and a celebration of two decades of music, resiliency, and reinvention.

Aguilera declared a fresh dedication to pursuing her individuality and pushing the limits of her work as she entered the next stage of her career. She freely discussed her continuous quest for self-awareness, her ambition to write meaningful music, and her commitment to sincerity in interviews. Aguilera's views on celebrity, artistic ability, and personal development had changed, and she was now more concerned with creating songs that spoke to her soul than she was with following trends or being a successful musician. Her priorities had been transformed by her experiences as a mother, artist, and campaigner, and she found fulfilment in endeavours that gave her the chance to be herself. Fans were inspired by Aguilera's changing attitude to her life and profession, which demonstrated to them that fulfilment and personal development are ongoing processes independent of notoriety or outward achievement.

The narrative of Christina Aguilera is far from done. She continues to be an important figure in the music business because of her unwavering devotion to her profession, her desire to pursue new creative endeavours, and her dedication to uplifting others. The world has learnt from Aguilera's path that reinvention is a constant process of development and discovery rather than a singular act. Her reputation as an icon and a role model has been solidified by her capacity to change while remaining loyal to her heritage and principles. Aguilera leaves behind a legacy of fortitude, genuineness, and self-determination as she goes on. In addition to inspiring admirers and other artists with her skill and creativity, she has taught them the value of being authentic in a society that often encourages uniformity. Future generations will be inspired by Christina Aguilera's path, which is one of bravery, growth, and creative integrity. The future is full with possibilities for her. Her narrative is still being told, whether she is performing, coaching, making music, or fighting for change. She contributes to her legacy with every new endeavour, serving as a reminder to the world that real icons are those who, in spite of all challenges, never stop evolving, inspiring, and reinventing themselves.

Chapter 7: Legacy and Lasting Impact

Christina Aguilera's voice has been characterised as one of the most powerful and flexible in the history of pop music. She has distinguished herself from her contemporaries with her unmatched vocal range and expressive delivery, earning her comparisons to such greats as Mariah Carey and Whitney Houston. Pop, R&B, soul, and Latin music are all dominated by Aguilera's vocal prowess, which cuts across genres. Her well-known songs, such as "Beautiful" and "Fighter," have become landmarks in both her career and music history. The music business has also been significantly impacted by Aguilera's vocal prowess. She raised the bar for what it meant to be a pop star by focussing on vocal delivery at a period when production and aesthetic appeal often eclipsed natural ability. Numerous musicians were influenced by her technical prowess and emotional depth, leaving a legacy that can be heard in the vocal styles of celebrities like Kelly Clarkson, Demi Lovato, and Ariana Grande. Aguilera demonstrated that a voice such as hers could endure in a trend-driven market.

Since its inception, Aguilera's career has served as a tribute to the genuineness and empowerment of women. Aguilera remained steadfast in her dedication to self-expression in a field that often puts pressure on women to live up to certain standards. By questioning conventional standards of beauty, sexuality, and self-worth, albums such as *Stripped* and *Bionic* encouraged listeners to value their uniqueness. By addressing themes of self-acceptance, gender equality, and perseverance in songs like "Can't Hold Us Down," "Beautiful," and "Fall in Line," Aguilera became an advocate for women and under-represented groups. Her audacious decisions, whether in her public remarks, clothes, or songs, inspired others to accept who they really were. By demonstrating to her audience that it's OK to be open, take chances, and demand respect, she established herself as an actual role model. Aguilera's impact went much beyond her music, spurring changes in societal perceptions of women's autonomy and self-expression. She has utilised her position to change the world, and her influence extends beyond the stage and studio. Numerous lives have been impacted by her activism and philanthropic efforts, which demonstrate her dedication to bringing about constructive change. Aguilera has continuously utilised her platform to inspire others, whether it be via her support of LGBTQ+ rights or her work with the United Nations World Food Programme. Her efforts on behalf of the LGBTQ+ community have been especially significant. Aguilera has been a vocal supporter of equality, devoting her shows and messages to her LGBTQ+ audience. She has been recognised with honours like the Human Rights Campaign's "Ally for Equality" award, which has strengthened her position as an advocate for love and acceptance. Because of her own hardships and experiences, Aguilera has also advocated for mental health awareness and anti-bullying initiatives. She is a relevant and inspirational character because of her candour about conquering personal obstacles, demonstrating that vulnerability and introspection are the keys to strength.

Christina Aguilera has shown a remarkable capacity to reinvent herself throughout her career. Aguilera has consistently changed while adhering to her basic principles, from the bubblegum pop of her debut to the raw and rebellious *Stripped*, the retro-glam of *Back to Basics*, and the contemplative artistry of *Liberation*. Every reinvention was a reaction to the rapidly evolving music business as well as a reflection of her own development. Her capacity to reinvent herself has impacted other performers, proving that staying relevant in the entertainment industry requires reinvention. She demonstrated how significant artistic achievements may result from taking creative chances and defying accepted conventions in the field. She is a pioneer who revolutionised what it means to be a pop star because of her unafraid attitude towards change and development.

Numerous modern musicians' careers bear the influence of Aguilera. Celebrities including Lady Gaga, Miley Cyrus, and Billie Eilish have praised her unreserved attitude to self-expression and dedication to her craft, citing her as an influence. Younger musicians that continue Aguilera's legacy of strength and creativity may be heard in their music, clothes, and live performances. Fans continue to find Aguilera's music and narrative to be very intimate. Her songs have acted as anthems for those going through difficult times, inspiring audiences to value their uniqueness and fortitude. Aguilera has established a relationship with her audience via her work that cuts across generations, leaving a lasting impression on people who look up to her.

Her narrative continues to be one of influence, resiliency, and change as she travels farther. To keep her fans interested, she has made references to upcoming endeavours such as additional songs, tours, and potential acting parts. Aguilera's path is far from done because of her determination to push herself and pursue new creative opportunities. The principles that Aguilera embodies—authenticity, self-determination, and the bravery to be oneself—are just as important to her legacy as her music. She has shown to the world that the most powerful voices are those who speak their truth and that genuine artistic expression originates from the heart. She has had an incalculable effect on pop culture, the music business, and her followers, and her influence will last for years to come.

Christina Aguilera's transformation from a gifted young singer to a worldwide music phenomenon is proof of the strength of fortitude, originality, and genuineness. Her narrative is one of shattering stereotypes, tearing down boundaries, and encouraging others to be themselves. As a reminder that the most lasting stars are those who shine by being completely themselves, Aguilera's legacy is one of empowerment. Christina Aguilera is a force to be reckoned with, a voice for change, and a testament to the timeless power of music and self-expression as she embarks on the next phase of her career.

Chapter 8: Cultural Impact and Global Reach

The impact of Christina Aguilera goes beyond her singing talent and financial success. Her capacity to shatter stereotypes in the music business has had a long-lasting impact on popular culture. By embracing her uniqueness and tackling difficult, sometimes controversial issues in her songs, she was among the first musicians to question the polished, conventional image of late 1990s pop singers. Aguilera created songs that were not just chart-topping blockbusters but also cultural landmarks, such as the celebration of inner beauty in "Beautiful," the raw vulnerability of "Hurt," and the female strength in "Can't Hold Us Down." She also stood out for her accomplishments as a multilingual. She paved the way for musicians experimenting with cross-cultural musical expressions with her early entry into Latin music with *1*Mi Reflejo* and her subsequent return to her origins with *La Fuerza*. Aguilera demonstrated how embracing one's origins might result in worldwide appeal by fusing Latin rhythms with her own flair. She became a worldwide advocate for cultural exchange because of her ability to transcend language and cultural barriers and show how music can bring people together.

Throughout her career, Christina Aguilera has expressed her changing personality and amplified her music via visual art and design. She became a trendsetter and cultural figure because of her chameleonic ability to change her appearance from the bubblegum pop diva of her debut to the edgy, confident artist of *Stripped*. Her *Stripped-era* style, which was defined by her daring attire, tattoos, and platinum blonde hair, served as an inspiration to many artists and came to represent revolt in the early 2000s. Her retro-glam makeover for *Back to Basics* also honored jazz and blues greats by fusing classic style with modern flare. Reinvention is a crucial element of cultural relevance, as seen by Aguilera's daring approach to style, which has impacted not just music but also fashion and beauty trends. Aguilera also defied social norms with her audacious decisions. Her support of self-expression and body acceptance inspired admirers to value their individuality. Aguilera remained steadfast in her message that beauty is varied and self-defined in a society that often chastised women for their looks. She became a symbol of empowerment for many who felt excluded or misunderstood because of her disregard of conventional conventions.

Christina Aguilera is one of the few musicians who has been able to connect with several generations. Aguilera's music, which tackled themes of love, self-discovery, and resiliency, served as a soundtrack to adolescence for those who grew up in the late 1990s and early 2000s. Later works like *Liberation* and *La Fuerza*, on the other hand, resonated with younger audiences and exposed her art to a new public. She has maintained her relevance in the digital era because of her presence on sites like Instagram and TikTok, where admirers post tributes, performances, and covers. These channels have also made her extensive catalog accessible to younger listeners, fostering a multigenerational fan base that honors her legacy. The impact of Christina Aguilera goes far beyond the US. Her music has been heard by people all around the globe, gaining her praise and loyal followers in many countries. From sold-out concerts in

Europe to her effect on the Latin American music industry, Aguilera has established herself as a worldwide phenomenon. Her popularity throughout the world has been further cemented by her philanthropic endeavors. Aguilera's role as an ambassador for the United Nations World Food Programme has brought attention to problems that impact millions of people globally, including hunger and malnutrition. Her commitment to make a positive influence outside of music is shown by her use of her platform for social good. Christina Aguilera's ability to adjust while maintaining her artistic integrity has guaranteed her continued relevance in a field where trends change often. She has influenced the course of mainstream music and society, not just changing with the times but also shaping them. Aguilera's career is proof of the strength of persistence, inventiveness, and honesty. Aguilera's impact will surely endure as long as up-and-coming musicians continue to look to her as an inspiration. Her readiness to take on significant challenges, honor uniqueness, and push the limits of performance and music has made a lasting impression on the globe.

It is impossible to overestimate Christina Aguilera's cultural influence. Millions of people have been moved by her activism, music, and image, transcending national boundaries. Aguilera's legacy is still a celebration of the beauty of self-expression, the transformational power of music, and the significance of being true to one's voice as she continues to create, perform, and inspire. Aguilera's transformation from a young woman with a dream from a tiny village to a worldwide celebrity serves as a reminder that genuineness, skill, and perseverance can make a big difference. Her legacy is one of perseverance, empowerment, and timeless creativity, and her narrative is a ray of hope for anybody who dares to dream.

Chapter 9: Influence on Future Generations

Aspiring musicians who want to successfully negotiate the intricacies of the music business while remaining loyal to themselves might use Christina Aguilera's career as a model. Her ability to combine technical proficiency, emotional depth, and a bold attitude to reinvention has made her a model for emerging artists. Her ability to integrate inspirations and transcend genres has taught musicians the importance of adaptability. She made it possible for singers like Lady Gaga, Dua Lipa, and Halsey to explore their creative limits without worrying about offending their listeners by demonstrating that they could strike a balance between popular appeal and artistic and personal expression.

Her support of female empowerment is among her most lasting contributions to popular culture. Early in her career, Aguilera asserted female independence in a field that has traditionally been controlled by male executives and producers. She inspired a generation of women to advocate for themselves by tackling topics like gender discrimination, sexual autonomy, and double standards in songs like "Can't Hold Us Down" and "Fall in Line." Numerous women were motivated to embrace their uniqueness and reject restrictive labels by her reluctance to fit in with society's expectations. Her bravery in addressing issues of body image, self-worth, and mental health gave many female musicians a platform on which to launch their careers. The self-assurance and independence of contemporary musicians like Lizzo, Billie Eilish, and Megan Thee Stallion, who continue her legacy of empowerment, are evidence of her impact.

Being an outspoken supporter of the LGBTQ+ community for a long time has greatly impacted Christina Aguilera's cultural influence. A rallying cry for self-acceptance, her hymn "Beautiful" was especially well-received by LGBTQ+ audiences. Aguilera is well-liked in the community because of her candid support and commitment to establishing secure environments for her followers. Her presence at Pride celebrations and vocal support of LGBTQ+ rights established a standard for musicians to utilise their platforms for activism. Younger artists like Troye Sivan, Lil Nas X, and Sam Smith have emulated Aguilera by promoting diversity in their public personas and embracing themes of love, acceptance, and pride in their music. Her method has established a standard for young singers, and her vocal talent is still unrivalled. Vocal instructors and music schools regularly examine her runs, phrasing, and expressive delivery as examples of brilliance in performance. Her impact on singers such as Ariana Grande, Demi Lovato, and Jessie J shows how widely her ability is admired. Many singers now want to emulate Aguilera's style of singing. Her ability to strike a balance between technical proficiency and sensitivity has motivated younger musicians to concentrate on their music's narrative elements in addition to vocal accuracy.

Aguilera's tale has important implications for musicians who want to keep control of their careers. Her resolve is shown by her readiness to stand up for creative freedom, even if it meant defying accepted conventions in the field. Records such as *Stripped* and *Bionic* were daring declarations that put genuineness ahead of fads. Her emphasis on taking control of her story encouraged other artists to follow suit. Aguilera's impact in valuing creative independence is shown in individuals like

Beyoncé, who produces very personal, self-directed projects, and Taylor Swift, who battled for control of her masters.

In addition to her influence on American pop music, Aguilera's success in other languages has served as an inspiration to musicians worldwide. She showed that cultural authenticity may lead to worldwide success by releasing *Mi Reflejo* and then going back to Spanish-language music with *La Fuerza*. Artists such as Shakira, Rosalía, and Karol G were inspired by Aguilera's work to embrace their heritage and engage with fans throughout the globe. Artists have been encouraged to explore cross-cultural collaborations by Aguilera's worldwide impact. Her ability to strike a balance between her Latin origin and her American pop identity demonstrated the unifying and bridging power of music. The legacy of Christina Aguilera extends beyond the honors she has accrued and the CDs she has sold. Her impact may be seen in the way artists approach their work, the dialogues they start with their artwork, and the acceptance and empowerment messages they convey to their audiences.

Aguilera's path offers guidance on how to handle celebrity, develop as an artist, and be true to oneself in a field that is always changing. Her experience demonstrates that genuine success is about producing work that has a lasting impact rather than focussing on short-lived success at the top of the charts.

The narrative of Aguilera is still important despite the way the world is changing. Fans and next generations of artists alike are inspired by her enduring music, activism, and fortitude. Her dedication to creativity, empowerment, and authenticity will guarantee that her legacy lives on, serving as a constant reminder to the world that those who dare to be themselves have the greatest influence. Christina Aguilera is more than just a legend to the next generation of musicians; she is a representation of what can be achieved when skill, willpower, and genuineness are combined. Through her music and her tale, she has given us a lasting reminder that genuine craftsmanship is not only about entertaining; it's about altering lives.

Conclusion

Christina Aguilera's transformation from a young woman from a tiny town with lofty aspirations to a global music phenomenon is a testament to her tenacity, willpower, and unwavering quest for authenticity. Her narrative exemplifies not just the strength of talent but also the bravery required to question conventions, value uniqueness, and utilize one's voice both physically and figuratively to spur change. She has redefined what it means to be a pop star and had a lasting impact on the music business. Her brazen attitude to self-expression has impacted several musicians, and her vocal range and creativity distinguish her as one of the best performers of her age. Aguilera has shown that music is a vehicle for empowerment, connection, and change in addition to being an entertainment medium via her revolutionary albums, advocacy activities, and unabashed individualism. Her influence goes much beyond her number-one singles. She has established herself as a voice for those who feel ignored because of her support of LGBTQ+ rights, female empowerment, and mental health awareness. By allowing her admirers to be really themselves, she has shown that genuine beauty is found in self-love and honesty.

Christina Aguilera is a timeless figure who has remained current for decades due to her ability to change while remaining loyal to herself. She has shown that reinvention is an art form as well as a survival strategy in the dynamic entertainment sector. Her story reminds us that greatness comes from accepting both successes and setbacks, and it is a ray of hope for those who are trying to leave their mark.

Aguilera's narrative is far from over as she keeps on advocating, inspiring, and creating. But one thing is for sure: her legacy will live on, inspiring future generations and touching hearts. The world is a better place because of Aguilera's voice, which is a testimony to the transformational power of being true to oneself in both music and life.

Printed in Dunstable, United Kingdom